Four Valley Poets

Four Valley Poets

Michael Marth
Terence Martin
A.C.L. Stanton
William Wallis

Introduction by John Zounes

STONE and SCOTT, *Publishers*
Sherman Oaks, California

Four Valley Poets

First Edition 1990

Printed in the United States of America.

Cover painting by Jack Seery.

Library of Congress
  Catalog Card Number 90-70715

ISBN 0-9627031-0-9

Contents

Preface

The idea for this book arose in a discussion in the English Department at Los Angeles Valley College. One person noted that e.e. cummings, John Dos Pasos, and six others had early publication in *Eight Harvard Poets* (Lawrence J. Gomme, 1917); another suggested that *Four Valley Poets* might modestly follow. Stone and Scott agreed.

Valley refers doubly to the college and to the area. Los Angeles *Valley* College is in the heart of the San Fernando *Valley*, a large portion of which is in the city of Los Angeles. The Valley was orchards and farms; then it was a bedroom for Los Angeles; now, it is the city John Zounes depicts in his introduction.

The poets are two teachers and two students at Valley College; three live in the Valley. They speak with their own distinctive voices and demonstrate that literary work is, indeed, produced *at* Valley (College) and *in* (the) Valley.

As a publication of Stone and Scott, the book, of course, has no official connection with or endorsement by Valley College. Stone and Scott do wish to express appreciation to staff and students who aided and encouraged in many ways.

Grateful acknowledgement is made to Martin R. and Rita Horn and to Dutton's Books whose support of the arts helped make this book possible.

Les Boston, Editor

Introduction:

Participation

The moment of change is the only poem.
—Adrienne Rich

More poetry. More light, dim or bright, more light. More human heart and heat. Wonderful. Enterprising people, poets: They go into business for themselves. They produce. Not for the marketplace, surely; no window in the Valley shopping malls advertises a post-holiday sale, a one-third off clearance, of contemporary poetry—unless it's that of a venerable Hollywood actor flashing his verse. Not for a beauty contest; no poet worth his or her salt writes or reads his or her work to pose the question, "Am I Ms. America yet?" or "Am I Mr. Wordly, wise and clever, or what?" At least we hope poets don't, but of course a few do. Nor do poets produce necessarily for an ideological forum, though if the poet's lines be useful, necessary, crucial—that is, political—by all means give that poet the lectern. And finally, if they are healthy in mind and spirit—most are, some not—poets do not compose themselves to be patted on the head and told what sensitive souls they are. They just write poems. Make stuff on their own. Every first poem ever written is the work of an amateur: A lover of some kind of someone or something. Strange creatures, these poets. Very human. "A touchy tribe," the old-timer Horace called them. Yes, in every sense of the word. *Toccatas.* Poets are people who, in Nikki Giovanni's words, "sometimes after midnight or just before / the dawn / . . . sit typewriter in hand / . . . to compose a poem / no one understands." Yes and no. Most of the simpler poems we readers understand right off. But some poems, even after a second or a tenth reading, it's true, we just don't understand: A whispered mystery going up in smoke, or a stone-worded labyrinth detoured enough to drive the reader mad. And yet, if the thing *is* a poem, and we live with it long enough, slowly, like life, slowly comes the dawn, the music and sense of it.

vii

Why, for heaven's sake, do they dabble in this sort of thing? Write poetry? Many try their hand at it for any and all of the reasons just mentioned. Others write poems because they have to, need to. They're drawn to the paradox: poetry is always everywhere, but most of the time almost impossible to find. Poet Wallace Stevens put it best: "Poetry is not a literary activity; it is a vital activity." But we're flapping our wings here: Any reader who has picked out this book and is thumbing the pages for samplings probably already knows what has just been said. Could we get to some specifics, please. **Four Valley Poets**? Poetry thriving here in the San Fernando Valley? A collector's item of sorts? Yes, certainly. A necessity of the Valley: more poetry.

The Valley, this sixth-largest city over the hill from the second-largest—soon to be *the* most congested—city north of the busy border; this materialistic mecca, this ghetto *cum* grotto, this bulldozed rolled-back real-estate temple of the drive-in drive-through drive-out life—poetry flourishes here? This landscape fashioned by the square root of what's here to-day and profitable tomorrow; this vast bedroom community where people work hard to raise children, forget children, combat insane traffic, avoid gangs, join gangs; where half the population goes to the movies and watches television as reli-giously as the other half dramatically prays; where people eat out at "in" places as often as possible, hang in, hang out, strive, hustle, listen keenly for opportunity's one knock, get up to answer the knock to cash in to be as middling as middle-class can be to finally get-away-from-it-all? Poetry lurks in these parts? Yes, here.

Scenes in the Valley still have the power to make us look twice, small reluctant reminders of why we live and work here: razored horizons in rare blue air (on rare blessed days), shy tract houses aproned with lawns manicured to putting-green perfection, block-long condos pretending they're Atticas on the Mediterranean, back alleys lined with trash and blazing bougainvillea, a tinted, gleamed limousine and a battered Dodge Ram pickup idling side by side egalitarian style at the stoplight, a heap of a homeless person waiting for that slow bus death at the same crossing, a string of blue palms on a violet and sure-to-be-violent somewhere summer night, and, every once in a while, the sight of kids of all colors playing tag on a school's asphalt yard. Pretty and too often not so pretty pictures. America compressed—Blake's Heaven and Hell. Promises half-made and half-kept. One wonders what Whitman would have made of the place, this Valley ("screaming electric, the atmosphere using / at random glancing, each as I notice absorbing / swiftly on"). It has almost everything, including poetry. Right under the nose, to the side of the eye; all one has to do is look for it. On college campuses, in church annexes, hip record stores, cafes, people's living rooms, bedrooms, vacant bank buildings on Saturday mornings, poetry is passed around. Good to know. Poets live here.

The trivia expert raises a point: How many poets live in the Valley? "Ahhhgh," that comic bard of the absurd, W.C. Dukenfield, would rasp back dead-pan, "Y'got me there." One figure in print estimates with surprising confidence that roughly forty million Americans write poetry or narrative of some kind. Another source claims there is one published poet for every one hundred thousand of this country's citizens. Go figure. Lawyers still—and probably forever will—outnumber poets, but the rumor grows that the number of poets is again on the rise. A good-news rumor, for a change. More poetry. The more poetry we get, the more good poetry we can choose for the bouquet, the centerpiece. Backtracking a few lines to that catch-all phrase, "of some kind," the next question is arguably not so trivial: Is what all these rising new poets write any good? Again, the response is no one really knows. Most poetry professors would understandably veto such an unprofessional, untutored, even unhinged notion, so let's rephrase that a bit more precisely: No one knows what someone *else* may like. Poetry, music, art—wonderfully democratic vistas. In these arenas, it is most emphatically a free country. Frost respected but didn't care much for Eliot's stuff. William Carlos Williams cringed at the sight of a sonnet (and ran off some beauties). Moore, Wilbur, and Ashbery are mandarins for those who prefer the more relaxed diction of, say, Sharon Olds, Lucille Clifton, Rita Dove. The many adopted children of Allen Ginsberg have little or no enthusiasm for poetry that doesn't remind them of Vallejo, Cesaire, Derek Walcott, Pablo Neruda. And so on. Go figure. Don't figure so far, however, that we advocate the notion: Abandon all judgment, ye who enter here. Not at all. We all have our aesthetic criteria, right down to the clothes we wear, but it seems best to leave judgment to the professional judges, the experts.

Just for the record, here are two of them. First, poet and poetry editor Donald Hall helps us to focus more tightly on this blurred idea of critical judgment hovering like a cloud over contemporary poetry: "If you write about Poetry Now, you must acknowledge that most of the poetry is terrible—most poetry of any moment is terrible. If you write an article claiming that poetry is in terrible shape, you are always right: Therefore you are always fatuous." Check. In fact, double-check. Let's try to skirt the fatuous here. The second helpful comment is from—you guessed it—another poet, James Dickey: "Though I have been made aware by my whole education of the necessity of internally consistent thinking and judgment, it appears to me that, where poetry is concerned, there are more important things than judgment involved, and that foremost among these is participation." I like that. And although Dickey, the sly connoisseur, does an about-face in his book *Babel to Byzantium* and offers almost three hundred pages of hard-headed critical judgments (some of them rather harsh) on poets, it's clear to the reader that Dickey the poet welcomes it all. "Where poetry is concerned," he welcomes all of it. Got it? Check.

Literature professors have a relatively easy task showing their poetry students what exactly they should sharpen their ears and eyes and minds for: To spot pretentiousness, sentimentality, predictability, and cliches—all the overweight or empty baggage of the human psyche. But it's another carousel altogether trying to sell students—or any readers of poetry—on what they *should* like. Just welcome it first. When it comes to taste, we literature teachers are something like good waiters; we recommend. Look, we work here, try this: It's delicate and elegant and true; or maybe this: It's raw and looks crude, but it's also true; it's all intelligent and new. Recommendations are, after all, almost as helpful sometimes in the Valley as hard currency: Fine restaurant; smart car on long-term appreciation; good investment, that location; and so on. Hold on there! Poetry isn't social chit-chat over lunch. Then again, maybe it should be. Anyway, I recommend **Four Valley Poets**, Michael

Marth, Terence Martin, A.C.L. Stanton, and William Wallis. They're a delight to read, and they offer some interesting, in spots some very fine, fare.

The lines in Michael Marth's work sometimes lurch around and bump into each other—perhaps intentionally so—but the persona is distinctive and likeable. Grizzled, gently gruff, he goes for the stoical aside that wants to sound both street-smart and country-bred. He is, in his own words, a dark-side prober and a doter on small successes, a chap who's been around the block a few times and knows that those small successes can often measure the quality of life better than the big win. Just knowing that can be a measure of success. Not trendy, of course, to dote on small successes this past decade and a half, but this writer does. And he does dote: He's excessively fond of those small creases among humans that don't get ironed out, unless in poetry—or in brawls, lawsuits, or silence. Better poetry. He searches along the shoreline of human relationships—with neighbors, friends, lovers, family, even strangers (poets have some of their best relationships with strangers)—to clasp and savor the memento: "bird songs, wet roofs, electric kisses, a perfect niche for my bicycle, a rabbit running by" on a night you're rolling in the grass.

Like Bukowski, to whom he alludes, Marth puts all his cards—high and low—on the table. And like Bukowski, Marth concedes he sometimes stretches it thin. Here's Bukowski on that note: "it is quite easy to appear modern / while in reality being the biggest damnfool ever born; / I know: I have gotten away with some awful stuff / but not nearly such awful pot as I read in the journals; / I have an honesty self-born of whores and hospitals / that will not allow me to pretend to be / something which I am not." It's the "honesty self-born" in Marth's lines that make many of them appealing, and a few questionable. Appealing, for this reader, when he's stretching to reach someone, himself included: Poems about drifting daughters, "grappling" sons, and sharing "unconditional love" with grandchildren expose Marth's persona at its gentlest and most winning. He'll risk sentimentality or even Ferlinghetti's "absurdity" to say just how he feels; you can trust him on that.

And that's a lot. Look twice at two of his poems, "They Call Me Papa" and "Growing Up in La La Land": In the first, that "rip-roaring" party and "dogs crawling all over me in 7th heaven" and "the children bring you their confidences knowing you will find them important" and "told a ridiculous story"—all that's authentic American quilt, Mark Twain in the stitching. Marth puts you there. In the second poem, he addresses a man, but "remembers" the man as a child, his son, and says eloquently, "i have no words i just try to hold him sometimes." Again, he puts you there and that "try" gives us pause, remembering ourselves. Marth's persona moves around nicely. He has a sense of the absurd ("the whole act clanking / and banging moves through something i don't understand") and of the comic (he manages to get himself locked out and finally reenters, Chaplinesque, "without a shred of decorum"). But he also says things such as "my vision has / always been of hosts of people / rising silently to tribute the / sun and living simply." Who says the sixties didn't offer a good year for wine? Forget the cliches; forget the lack of punctuation that disguises patches of prose; we'll even forget that "fallen over" bong: You can party with this man and feel comfortable.

"Comfortable" is not a word that pops to mind reading Terry Martin's work. It's on edge. A nice probing edge. It does what good writing is supposed to do sometimes: Make the reader a little nervous. Reading Martin is like being stranded on the road, forced to hitch a ride, and along comes this erratic driver who offers you a trip along with the ride. You didn't want the trip, just the ride, but you realize that they're one and the same, so you sit back and enjoy both—since he's going your way and is willing to tell you some fishing stories in the bargain. "Erratic" in the sense that Martin's lines have a curious, almost offbeat, feel to them. He cruises at a slow, deliberate speed along the straightaway—the narrative line—and then revs up to seventy into the curve—not just *before* the curve, *into* the curve. The reader feels the centrifugal pull of the ground before the mind registers the speed of the dash. It puts you on edge. And it can be exciting. There's a voice developing here—a definite style of pushing the words and ideas to see what they can do. Unlike Marth, whose persona seems content to wait for the "veil" to part and the "magic" to come, and who states flat out "i don't know who i am," Martin seems to be slipping through gears, accelerating from "I don't know either" to "But I'm damn well going to find out."

That nice edge—the tension—comes from Martin's working with contraries, opposites, surfaces and their reflections ("Dr. Jekyll's Confession," "Roommates," "Concentrics," even that "Landlord," who "died thirty years ago"—a literal figure shuffling around, or the poet himself being a custodian of his past?). Actually two voices are usually meshing into the one persona. A line from Dylan Thomas is a helpful road sign here: "I, in my intricate image, stride on two levels, / Forged in man's minerals, the brassy orator / Laying my ghosts in metal." When Martin is busy laying his ghosts—having some fun with Dracula and Narcissus ("The Transylvanian feels he deserves / Some sort of identity"), "feeling the taste / Of my darker self / Sliding down my throat," or being fully preoccupied with two mistresses, one in the closet and one in the bed—that's when he's cruising the narrative line; the road's a straightaway, but Martin keeps snaking from one lane to the other because that's where the story is. Clever self-searching stuff. The trip with the ride. But it's when Martin turns his attention to those "intricate details"—when he speeds up into those short, blind curves—that the reader stares hard at the text. A Zen touch: to speed through stillness. To sit in a disabled car and notice "a bird heads south" freely; the bird becomes a compass of the emotions. Enough said. Or double-check the closing lines of "Lunch Counter": "and Oh my dear / it is from the sadness / of cups, the silence / of plates that we / must keep each other." Wonderful. It's like hearing a young Ella Fitzgerald reciting an aging Theodore Roethke. Or, what could be viewed as the stunner of the bunch: "Found Poem." There are, I think, three or four poems teasing the imagination under the surface of this one short poem. The reflection of the self, the not-self, the mortal, the mundane, the evanescent—the mind talking to the brain: the perception of the ghost-concept and in the perceiving, the concept dissolves. Poetry. Speeding *into* the curve. Martin's best lines have that ghost-text. "To be fenced alone in Azusa / Standing beneath a billboard / Of a twenty-foot plastic / Neon trout." To be stuck—where was it? Someplace around Mobile with—what was it?—something like those Memphis blues again? Complementary lines from the same soil. Complimentary.

The springiness—the febrile kick—in Martin's lines comes from his trying to freeze what's *not* there; in still-lives, he finds mental landscapes ("the rumble of dust," "each blade of grass flinches," "the closing circle" of ivy, "A roomful of eyes saying jump," and, straight out of Thomas (not Tom) Wolfe: "She knows how it feels to see / Everyone in the world / Only once." And then nothing there: that empty space, waiting to be filled again. An American bent. Marth, Martin, Wallis—all three in the middle of the American grain. Not nostalgic, not sentimental, but a little *possessed* either by what isn't quite real or something larger than life, or by something that once was but is no longer there: parents, childhood, family love, innocence, simplicity. The American grain starting to weather. Who made the world so complex all of a sudden? Who left the apple pie out in the acid rain? "The land was ours before we were the land's" is the well known opening line from Frost's poem "The Gift Outright." And critic Lionel Trilling has suggested disturbingly that Frost, that icon of solid Americana, is "a terrifying poet." And there is something "terrifying" about much American poetry with its looking for lost fathers, lost loves, a long gone way of life. The American pilgrim: half puritan, half romantic. Still caught between what's here one moment in life and gone the next.

Ann Stanton will have none of it, or none of it without a peppering of wit. Not that her work doesn't focus on loss or death; on the contrary, of the four poets presented here, she seems the most conversant with the idea of something or someone gone. But it's her angle of vision that's different. Her work is that of the realist—the matter-of-fact empiricist—who looks squarely at what *is* there and comments on it. She makes the most eye contact; she looks at the idea, the thing, the feeling, and then tells the reader just how she responds to it. The subjective, the fanciful even, are of course present in her work, but they don't get any priority; it's what's out there that matters to her. Death, injustice, beauty, brutality, the almost-born—whatever her subject, her gaze is unflinching, steady, sure. As she says, she chooses, even in the most anguished setting, "the full experience." Carrying a child she describes as "feeling tides turn and my small ocean's roll"; on the threshold of delivery, she addresses the baby with "The hardest [work] we'll ever do"; then, only at the end of the poem does the reader realize how deeply the irony of that line cuts. But she's strong, feisty, this mourner of dead seals, lame pigeons, beaten-to-death humans; they'll have to "whack" the last breath out of her, if she has any choice in the matter. (Does anyone out there remember Edna St. Vincent Millay: "I shall die, but that is all I shall do for Death"?) And Stanton's fancy is agile and dexterous enough to get inside a voyeur of a cat (a literal Peeping Tom?) on a mantle, spying on the family dogs, the family itself, the images on the television set; the graceful feline—with its tail "a scepter, a plume, conductor of symphonies"—takes full assessment of the scene and decides it's the only cultured aristocrat in the room. Stanton gets inside the head of a young Queen Christina of Sweden, who gets catty with the French Queen Mother: "Ignoring her dried amethyst, veiny claw, I sought her gimlet eyes instead"; she romps a bit as *Dona Quixote*, asking, "has some knave tied a knot in my lance?"

Obviously there are humor and spirit here, a love of puns and other wordplay and sarcasm. (Of the four poets, Stanton displays, for me, the most sheer pleasure in words as words, the fun to be had with them; hers is a modern-day Elizabethan gusto; the words come almost too trippingly in some of her lines.) When she chooses to be spare and economical, Stanton serves up images that stay with the reader long after the poem is read: the evangelist who appears "trussed up sugared / half-baked ham"; "the death of a giant . . . a fluorescent pinwheel"; the Hotel del Coronado as "The Last Resort," where "palm trees—like the tails of lions—stiff as boards" and "lions there guard an ancient tomb, a treasure trove of doubloons and doilies." With that last poem she skewers the mummified ambience of that ramshackle "Gatsbian" joint. But it is the poem "Colored Lights" that is, I think, her *piece de resistance*. This poem is a dancing winner. Everything—every word—falls into perfect place. On the surface it is a mash note to actor Marlon Brando, and only readers who can go back in that actor's career to the Nebraska and New York City days of

"Bud" Brando can savor the multiple meanings of the punch-line. From that "insinuating . . . Body" that "honkey-tonked" in the early days, down to the "gristle and fat" of the present and then back again, Stanton flickers that enigmatic celebrity like a Javanese shadow play in her mind's eye perfectly. There's a ghost text here: That's what makes it a fine poem—not that its subject is an actor. The spaces in the text comment silently on the real beauty of youth, on living a life of various roles, aging, and then viewing youth again from the perspective of matured experience. All of it dramatic, all of it "colored lights." An elegant cameo.

Reading Bill Wallis is a little like watching the needle tremble on a seismograph: there's a fault down there grinding its plates; the tremors are just perceptible enough to make you unsteady, and you keep waiting, expecting the earth to move. And it does. Not under your feet, though, but around your head. Wallis can make your head spin with the very intensity of his pronouncements. In Wallis's work, we're getting into rarefied territory. An assault on the transcendent. An attempt to burn a hole in the page, or to make that needle slide all the way off the graph. The reader, this one at least, needs a hand strap, a railing, something to hold onto for balance. A hint of Blake ("O holy child!"), of Hopkins (counterpoint rhythms), of Rilke, of many literary influences, but Wallis's unique voice is always prominent, a voice that likes to wrap itself in rhetorical closure, ideas, correspondences. This last term—borrowed from literary criticism—implies, roughly, a fusion between the physical world and the spiritual realm (Baudelaire: "Everything, form, movement, number, color, perfume, in the spiritual as in the natural world, is significative, reciprocal, converse, *correspondent*"). The natural world is a mystical index feeding images into the mind's (or the soul's?) monitor, which, in turn, transforms them into transcendent values. Wallis soaks his imagery in this reciprocal turn of mind. Eroticize the spiritual, spiritualize the erotic: poems such as "Landscape," "Song," "Cadillac," are occasions for sex to be experienced as a baptismal font, a communal rail, a kabalistic text, in short, as a religious experience. And, one hopes, as sex.

Much of Wallis's work—"All Sons," "Dream Son," "Before Sunrise,"—is appreciated easily enough: paeans to family life, his son, fatherhood, the act of love; "the dark chuckle of touch"—a wonderful line—tells us just how the poet feels about touching.   If, however, the reader has a little difficulty penetrating some of Wallis's more opaque lines, it is, I think, because they're not meant to be transcribed into everyday thought: rather, like skin, just tasted, touched, absorbed. There are still mysteries in life, after all. (Rilke: "How he gave himself up to it. Loved. / Loved his interior world, his interior jungle, that primal forest within, on whose mute overthrownness, / green-lit, his heart stood. Loved.")

The intensity with which Wallis examines the stories of his unique interior world—a whole cosmos of dreams, memories, emotional peaks—urges, literally *urges* readers to delve more deeply into their own unique interiors. Because he can create these dreamscapes, there is, except for one or two poems, no ghost-text in Wallis's work; he's too busy grappling with his personal vision of the Holy Ghost, trying to synthesize memory with something like infinity, trying to make emotions incarnate and ideas pregnant with feeling. He's drawn to music, to jazz musicians. (Try reading his poem "Pacific Coast Fragments" or "Caliban" aloud with John Coltrane's "Ascension" playing mutely—if that's possible—in the background, and you get a better idea of what Wallis is after on paper—controlled frenzy or disciplined exuberance or something along those lines.) He wants the enthusiasm to breathe on the page. To say Wallis is drawn to music is to understate the case: "I cannot imagine existence without song," he writes elsewhere.   Many of Wallis's lines create the vivid impression that the poet is engaged in, not just literary activity, but a vital activity; that the form and harmony of music and poetry will—must—bestow order upon the world. At least the world as this particular poet sees and feels it. One poem is quite graceful in its subtle play of ideas: "In the Theater." This short piece resonates with all the qualities found in Stanton's "Colored Lights." The performer, the accompanist, the orchestra, the audience all meld into making life gloriously alive and quick. Is the poem about a musical performance? About lovemaking? About the writing of poetry? About the joy of it all? The answer is Yes. Wallis's intense, enveloping tone calls to mind a writer (also a poet) best known for his novel *A Death in the Family*. James Agee's preface to that book, entitled "Knoxville: Summer 1915" (made music by Samuel Barber) is lyrical, robust, written with a youthful voice that sounds ultimately responsive to and responsible for almost everyone and everything loved that passes in the world. Wallis can give you an echo of that. He gives some light to the dark places of existence. And he celebrates the wonder of it. We can always use more of that.

But all the commentary may be redundant; poets are their own best introduction. Enjoy.

John Zounes

Poems by

Michael Marth

The Arrangement

He wanted her to be an airline stewardess
or an executive secretary or a nurse
she does a 5-9 gig at the meat rack
dancing with less than he's seen her in
and he says nothing
it's hardly either's expectations

it's been bad between us but she was
genuinely charming when she talked about
it   like she'd discovered a concerned
listener in her life for the first time

i don't wear string bikinis   they seem to
prefer a little more   it makes them imagine
they can see something i guess   it was cynical

i wanted to tell her keep your sense of art and person
don't start hating men and don't depreciate your
own passion   but i said nothing

so her dad picks her up every night growling at
hustlers and remembering when she was an armful
of love with chicken pox just 23 years ago
and both have a little trouble falling asleep.

Pressing On

The bong fell over
it's that kind of night
why am i beating my brains out
when i could be somebody of
fry cook creativity where
what i made would be felt

i'm going through the motions of being
golf monday   basketball wednesday
shower three times a week
and suddenly nowhere
begging and baiting
and so far down

lucky for me the tease of tv
rarely reaches anymore
oh i still lust after a
heroine with hooters once
in awhile or the glamorous
new buick
friends say with your way with
words why don't you get into

advertising or greeting cards
but i know i'm a better writer
than a normal decent person
and i probe the experience
of the dark side nobody wants
to hear and dote on small
successes that translate hell
into humanity and bind my
stuff into books meaningless
in my time if not forever
and try not to wonder why.

The Mirage

Alive in all the yards of concrete
that surround me are a half mile long
row of flowering street trees that
strangely have no smell and the lawns
of the office high rise

they are an effect i drink

if my bike tires are flat i walk
and relish the chug-a-chug of the
rainbirds giving water to this
scene so lost to the central city

i saw a bee in one of the trees
the other day confused about
whether or not his
raison d'etre was here

i know how he feels.

Growing Up in La La Land

It's hard to see my son get older in the sense
that he thinks the world is falling apart
that only money counts and that he must try to
tell his kids what diminished quality
of life they can expect

it's good perhaps that he grapples
that there's a new set of hands at the
work   that he cares

i remember like it was yesterday when
he woke in the night crying out and his
mother or i would comfort him

i remember the beautiful hopeful poem
he wrote at six and the courageous way
he responded to what must have been an
horrendous earthquake to him

i remember him graduating from marine
boot camp charged up to kill something
and the long subsequent descent from that
consciousness and all marine solutions

and so we have a gentle man reluctant
to tear out someone's heart for a bmw who
sees corruption and incompetence all around him

and i have no words   i just try to hold him
sometimes and assure him he's in a period of
awareness   still crying out in the night
and not alone.

Nature

The whisper of a new day coming
is punctuated by a bird song
wet roofs testify to dew from
a sky open to outer space
you can almost hear the trees leave

babies are being born who will
inherit all this meaning for themselves
and lovers roll into each other asleep
and make more

it's there   it's always there
the beauty against the clanking
and roar and pall of progress

some say we are doomed for our
excesses   but my vision has
always been of hosts of people
rising silently to tribute the
sun and living simply

one day we will face that choice
and live rather than avoid death
the spirit exists to rediscover
our humility   perhaps it only
waits for catastrophe or a new
consciousness

i favor the latter.

Bullish

The roar of a
power mower chases the muse
the birds
and stray cats
on the prowl
for a meal

soon it will
be followed by
the shriek of a
power blower which pushes half
the cuttings back
into the grass

they can stubble
the lawns but
they can't stop the
leaves from falling
and i found several
piles this morning
i could kick up in
the air and scatter
and i didn't feel
bad at all
hell i was
creating jobs.

Give Me Your Tired . . .

You can't put it there
i didn't recognize the accent but i
had just ridden five miles for a prescription
because i had no money for the bus
and i found a perfect niche for my bicycle
in front of this massive office building
in the middle of nowhere
out of everyone's way and was going to run in
and grab a pack of smokes on the cuff from
the lobby concession of a friend

you have to go on to the lot in
back where the motorcycles park
i still couldn't place the accent
i was inside 60 seconds and came out
unlocked my bike and started toward
the toll booth

the attendant could see i wasn't going
to stop and threw down the barricade
you owe me 70¢ he screamed   i squeezed
between the curb and the end of the
barrier without even slowing
realizing the scam

and they come here from all over the
world with the fever.

They Call Me Papa

It was a rip roaring birthday party
two sons and a daughter-in-law   celebrating
rock n' roll on the radio   laughing   joking
a drinking game to see who tossed first
and me with grandchildren and kittens and
dogs crawling all over me in 7th heaven

there's something special about being a
grandfather   the children bring you their
confidences knowing you will find them important
and sharing unconditional love   you don't
care if their hands are dirty or their shirts
on backward or they broke the last crystal
water glass climbing on the sink or had a
little blow up and voiced anger

they sit your knee and put an arm
around your neck and suddenly impulsively
hug and look at you like you're someone

and you don't have to be a football hero or
score with women   well   maybe one
or knock down 6Ok a year or even be a
good poet

and when i'd tucked them in bed and told
a ridiculous story and wished them good
dreams and said i love you i returned to
the revelry and using moves from the
soul i danced the night away

hey   grandfathers do that too.

Another Drum Silenced

A thousand phrases come to me that fit my life
snatches of songs that celebrate love and loss
and hope and resignation to a tide of events
over which there seems such small control
poems that speak the glory of being and the
inevitability of surrender   lines of stories
that exult in triumph and parallel my failures
a thousand answers to questions i don't know how
to form out of a swirl of desperate seeking

inspiration efficacy immortality riches
inner peace a connection with the pervasive
spirit or a good cheeseburger an electric
kiss a tender understanding self worth
a hearty lengthy laugh to mock my sobriety
what will satisfy this indefinable hunger

my friend howard an award winning writer
literate and smart simply gave up poetry
and started submitting articles to motorcycle
magazines   he hasn't sold but he says he's
happy   he plans to become a bartender.

Exposed

Coffee
cigarettes
pot
booze
food additives
pesticides
paint
hairspray
salt
glue
drugs
patent medicines
electric shock
radiation
and sex
destroy brain cells

i haven't started
to drool yet
or forgotten
my shoes
but it's only a
question of time.

The End

It'll be a cool morning hush
on the lake in the woods
and i'll look out the porch screens
and smell the day

an expiring june bug
whirls and clatters
and a chattering chipmunk
gathers what he must

deep darkening clouds
rise from the valley
they say the fish bite
like crazy when it rains

the sea runs quiet   stretching
forever from this mountain top
and the brewing coffee intoxicates

and she shows in a robe she drops
and slips into my arms
e. power biggs is playing poulenc

then they can have me for mink food or whatever.

The Price of Curiosity

Eight o'clock in the morning
and some idiot is running what
sounds like a power mower in the hall
my tongue feels like something
i should spit out and my eyes hurt
i'm dressed in shorts and sox

i open the door   the custodian
is vacuuming the hall
i mumble something about the
trash chute floor being littered
he investigates and it's been
cleaned up   he knocks on my
door to tell me and in disbelief
i go to see for myself   letting
the door slam

now i'm locked out and of course
everyone but the miss america
pageant comes by before finally
he returns with the keys and
when i get back in it's without a shred
of decorum

none of my philosophy covers this
and i realize that the tides of
fortune simply claim us and our
dignity and i chuckle at the
spontaneity that still makes life
leveling and scald my tongue into
submission with hot coffee.

After the Play

So many hands around the back
on the arm   shaking my hand
so many good looking women
in arousing dresses

i love that joke
i still get aroused
but i forget why

so many hugs in one night
the theater crowd is warm
but i frightened at least
one girl looking down her decolletage

i patted no asses
i'm proud of myself
i didn't snatch any beauties
and throw them over the
refreshment table in a
mad passionate kiss
i didn't offend any escorts

i cried once
and got so scared
i fled into a hiding place

on the way home waiting
on the bus bench i checked
out a braless brazen honey

you could see everything
and she smiled as i stared

it was a hell of an evening.

The Passing Parade

She was in a bra and panties the
first time i saw her   her boyfriend
left us alone in her kitchen
to sing a song she did cutely
while he went out for beer

when she finished she smiled
sat down   devoured a cigarette
got up   put on her shorts
walked out on the porch
and screamed i want money

she was wowing them some
time later when we had dinner
but amazingly she was more naked
never stopping moving
showing you everything and nothing

she went on to become a star
what else i remember of her was
she too thought i was slow
there must be some truth to it.

Limitations

I gnaw a bloody knee in my dream
i will have my rage
confront the whole damned world
savage as a rogue ape
scream my crudities

but so must i always petition
the god in me for validation
that ever moving center that
softly appears in my mind
forgiving the ugliness of
a day with a gentle touch

hell i'm a whore and a clown
and a wimp and a bully
a tyrant   a penitent

and the whole act clanking
and banging moves through
something i don't understand

my own higher purpose.

Civilization

One more time
penetrate the veil
and bring back magic

the night lies like a
garbage can cover on the city
no stars   no moon
a radio distorts its message
and the goddamn refrigerator grinds

why is life made up of
so many tedious moments
why don't i get up and do
something about it

morning's first light appears
soon the town will throw
its feet on the floor
and a million cars will turn
left at the same time
what if they turned right
one wonders.

Balance

Do you mind if I fart I ask
as i knock the contents of the
coffee table askew
the place needs cleaning
i haven't got the price of a drink

she thinks it's wonderful i reach
out to her   but occasionally i
gotta have somebody around

i light up another hit of pot
and she complains   but i don't listen

she's as desperate as i am
for company
i don't like myself at times
but i love myself at others

maybe it all works out.

The People's Voice

On a street light pole in front of a
chinese restaurant down the block
someone with a poetic sense spray painted
UCLA mocking the circumstances that
would never see him in that school on
his way to leadership and fortune and
privilege

some powerful statements are made
in graffiti   one of my favorites was
in the bowels of the barrio   where sex
and life are cheap   and the currency
is food stamps and drugs   and despair
is a presence like a winter morning fog

it said WIN.

A Twist

Poet charles bukowski's
got it down
it's so goddamned easy
hating everybody
no excuses
no conflicts
no trying to perform to the
expectations of goodness

and so being
the very thing he's laughed at
he's achieved
making it

it's all kinds of
wonderfully perverse
like life is.

In Touch

O let me ride the night
to a place in the mind
where the cherry blossom
smell drifts in the air
and fireflies rise
in the fields
and you roll in the grass
and get high going over and over

there are so many stars
you feel like you're surrounded
and the dark is bright
enough to see a rabbit run by
it's just natural being
part of the miracle

life like the river runs on and on
and poetry manifests itself everywhere
not the least in the freedom
one feels in his associations

of course the visit is fleeting
but the farther i get from
my childhood the greater
the magic seems and somehow
the closer.

Poems by

Terence Martin

Be quiet and go angling.
—*The Compleat Angler*

Walton's Thumb

Be patient
until the evening distances
the drone of the last boat.
Wait
while flies scramble like commuters
for the final shafts of sun.
When your hand rises in its shadow
Present the lure
it flutters into life
dances on the lake
disappears
like a word
cast upon silence.

Dr. Jekyll's Confession

A lot like you,
I am afraid of my own
Shadow, so I drink—
Feeling the taste
Of my darker self
Sliding down my throat
Like a snake
Regretting the loss
Of its own skin.
I drape my arm
Across the lab table
As if it were a bar,
Behind which could stand
A bartender who polishes
Test tubes and nods
Understandingly.
I remember only vaguely
The creature who scurries
Through my dreams,
But each morning
my eyes feel heavier—

Two dark stones
Tied to the face
Of a drowning man
And in my mouth a faint
Taste of salt water,
Perhaps of tears.
No wonder
I have kept my shadow
A safe distance behind me.

Roommates

Due to a severe housing shortage
Dracula and Narcissus, unable
To get work, have become
Roommates. The Count sleeps throughout
The day, while his Greek friend
Spends his time staring into the
Mirror. But lately Narcissus
Has had the disturbing feeling
That the face in the mirror
isn't really his own. Familiar, yes.
But different. In fact,
The opposite of what it should be.
Whenever he frowns, his double
Seems to grin like a fiend,
The corners of the mouth
Breaking into a rictus
Of uncontrolled laughter and
When Narcissus smiles, his
Counterpart grimaces
In a vaguely uneasy way.
So he stands, sometimes
For hours, trying to figure it out.

***

Dracula has begun to notice
His friend's preoccupation,
And now, late at night
The caped man slips into
The bathroom to see what obsesses
The Greek to such a degree.
But he doesn't see what the problem is.
There is nothing, in fact,
In the mirror. Nothing but
The room where his face
Should be, only the sad
Bodies of objects, the chair
Getting soft at the middle,
The comb, lying on its side,
Sprouting grey hair like an old man.
Even the chrome fixtures
refuse to acknowledge him.

***

Now the roommates have begun
To resent each other. They spend
hours arguing. Each believes
His own situation is worse.
The Transylvanian knows he deserves
Some sort of identity, that even pain
Is an improvement over immortality.
The Greek is sick of seeing
Exactly what he is not.
Their lights burn late into the night,
From their rooms, the sounds of desperate
Voices, and of glass, breaking.

Fuel Stop on 395

The sign on the roof declares
LAST CHANCE
To this place which doesn't exist
On maps, they arrive for the ritual
Of stretch, gas and window cleaning.
The attendant is bored, his faded
Blue overalls too short
Above shoes the anonymous
Color of oil and leather.
He cleans windows in his sleep
And tries to sell his house
To anyone in full serve.
His sister sits in a cage
Of glass, measuring time
By the gallon. She dreams
Of departures and wheels
Whispering her name. She knows
How it feels to see
Everyone in the world
Only once.

Buffalo

In my life
I have had three encounters
With buffaloes.
The first was white,
From an episode of Rin Tin Tin
I can barely remember.

The second was a painting
In blues and black
Done by my father
Who recognized too late
What was looming
From some dark prairie
Within him.

The third was a dingy brown
Real buffalo
On the outskirts of L.A.
Penned between
A herd of dairy cows
On one side
And Happy Jack's Fish Farm
On the other.
He stands alone
All day watching the cars
And the unsuccessful fisherman
Stopping for something to take
Home to the wife and kids.
He is
Harassed by real flies.

Perhaps this is
The price buffaloes pay
For our childhoods
And our darkest fears:
To be fenced alone in Azuza
Standing beneath a billboard
Of a twenty-foot plastic
Neon trout.

Koala and Kangaroo

How reassuring for marsupials.
To rest in a pouch with a great
Tit in your mouth.
Nothing to do
But suck and contemplate
Whether or not you want to get up
That day. If you do leave
The warmth of your furry house
And things don't work out
You can always return home.

Today after entering
The zoo through
The one-way turnstile
In a herd of humans
I stood in a crowd three deep
Craning necks to watch
A koala awake in false
Darkness, staring back and
Chewing on a leaf.

Tonight I'll sleep in real
Darkness and dream of a cage—

Above it a plaque
With my name in Latin.
It's lined with books
And furniture and visited
By a keeper who brings
Cigarettes and coffee twice a day.
It's up past the existential zoo
With empty cages full
Of extinct animals.

Later I'll wander up there
And give in to this irresistible urge
To crawl inside my own pockets.

Poetry 212   MWF 9:00

Today they discuss
How hard the age has been
On poets—
                          Crane and Kees
Their water routes
Each to his own south.
                          Berryman
Tumbling through lunatic air
Past his father's body.
                          Randall Jarrell
Silhouetted into mere print
By the headlights' glare.

Afterwards, a student in the back
Proposes that they must have been
"Accident prone."
                          Perched on the edge
Of his desk the teacher
Stares beyond the window
A roomful of eyes saying jump.

for lou reed and bob dylan

maybe it's a form of chronological
                    homesickness
whatever it is it's not
                    alonesickness
i've got plenty of friends
                    but they're acting old
watching kasey kasem
                    listening to solid gold
radio   oh no could that be me
                    let's see
i'm hunting grey hairs
                    like they were in season
oh no   there must be
                    a reason
look out ma it's something you did
the war is over let's have a kid
i'm not saying i was born too late
                    i was born too soon
why couldn't you wait
                    why couldn't you wait
why couldn't you wait
                    i've got a woman at home
who sings love is strange
                    while she combs her hair
i call her sylvia
                    her name is jennifer

but she doesn't care
                she says lou lou lou

you're the last great american poet
                writing on napkins

sitting in bars this oral
                tradition doesn't go far

passing it on and passing out
                and she says without a doubt

you're the last great american poet

you're the last great american

you're the last great

you're the last.

His Mistress

You found her picture in the trash
Naked and stupidly discarded
In pieces. You reassembled her
Like a laboratory monster,
Your polaroid demon
Summoned into 5 x 7 flesh.

Now she hangs in your closet
Pinned into the hem of a formal
Her glossy skin naked against
Your pink satin dress.

Your husband works late at the restaurant
Brings home leftovers in the back seat
And keeps a gun in the glove box.
He has, he says, a lot on his mind.

A night does not pass
Without you slipping from bed
To take her out and hold her
In your hand. Then you tuck her in
And turn out the light
As she sleeps in your girlhood
A few feet away.

Lunch Counter

Throughout the meal
and after, each eye
fastens to some object:
cream warming in
the ridiculous cow-
shaped dispenser,
smudge of catsup
on last year's calendar,
coffee cup tilted
in its saucer.
We cut our teeth
on cups like these.
The careless wear
of lips has smoothed
their edges and Oh my dear
it is from the sadness
of cups, the silence
of plates that we
must keep each other.

Concentrics

The ivy in our backyard
grows in contrary directions:

It climbs the brickwall
clings to the sill
settling into space,
the other side.

It crawls too toward the center
in a closing circle
seeks itself across the garden

Where summers, we settle on lawn chairs.
Sipping drinks, we watch
the radius of our world
grow smaller.

detail

a bird heads south
across the closed grey
window of a car
pointing north
sagging westward
on one flat tire

Sky Water

Leaves in the shapes of birds
Float south for the winter.
Orange words on blue paper.

beneath those wrinkles
she is white
as a china cup
soft as old teeth
her eyes
will grind you up
either
spit you out
like a bad taste
or swallow you
like a long lost son.

The Landlord

died thirty years ago.
that hasn't stopped him
from making his rounds
the same each day
down the driveway
across the lawn
past the closed mouths
of mailboxes and garbage cans,
circling like a confused vulture
looking for a sign of life
talking to anything that moves.
as he shuffles by
each blade of grass flinches
pretending not to grow.

Found Poem

objects in
the mirror
are closer
than they
appear

silence is only as still

as the air within a bell

that remembers the hourly gesture

and the echo of footsteps

shuffling flights below—

the rumble of dust

settling on cement

Last night
In the shower
I overheard
The last two movements
Of Shubert's Unfinished.

That missing
Play of Sophocles
Turned up
Under my kitchen table.

Later
I had a dream
And remembered
What Coleridge forgot.

This morning I wrote
A 2 line haiku
And a 13 line sonnet.

Somebody
Is trying to tell me something.

Poems by

A.C.L. Stanton

The Impatient Tree

Stripped bare by February,

the long thin bony fingers

admonish the clarity of the sky.

A sabbath wind lingers to visit a while

and the spindly fingers

claw at the cloudless Sunday blue.

Squirrels' nests of dried, impacted leaves

hanging on for dear life,

webbing the longest fingers,

are all that remain of summer's finery.

Impatient for spring,

the long, thin, bony fingers,

some artistically twisted,

others arthritically bent,

begin a nervous drumming against the winter sky.

Tar Pits

The cars whizzed by yet he stood his ground in the street
like a fool, not taking startled, sensible flight.
My mind composed a hasty string of
angry, anxious adjectives:

> Stupid, arrogant, silly pigeon,
> Bold and brazen, crazy gray slate bird!

He remained, leaning, listing, one wing poised oddly,
like a sassy hand on a flippant hip,
a belligerent, loitering, nose-thumbing pose.
> The car behind mine was framed in my rearview
> mirror
> and it passed him as closely as I,
> and still he wouldn't fly.
I drove on, remembering the snarled, stalled traffic
on this recently widened street
> and I suddenly knew it had been finally tarred
> this day.

Executing an illegal U-turn, I sped back,
hearing myself breathe,
swearing out loud, pounding the wheel,
feeling in my bones the ache of one more lost cause.

> Damn nitwit birdbrain, I scolded,
> Couldn't you have stayed in the park
> on top of a statue
> where it is still possible for you to belong?

A double row of cars faced me at the corner
where there had been but a single file moments before.
Only the freshly tarred surface was crisscrossed with tire marks
now, pockmarked with one flattened bird of extinction.

And I think of the Tar Pits of La Brea
of the creatures who came to slake their thirst,
to nibble on tender shoots, on manzanita and
elderberry—some of them,
or on each other—some of them.
Slowly, by agonizing inches, they sank into the ponds,
the saber tooth, dire wolf, sloth,
the short-faced bear,
into the black ooze beneath.
Roaring, whimpering, struggling, at first,
communally dying, converged, at last.

Then I moved forward slowly as the light turned green,
the Volkswagen behind me honking impatience
at my Cougar's funereal pace.

Montezuma's Revenge
(or How To Become a U.S. Marine)

Bumbling, snotty, slowpoke kid
molasses witted misfit,
shut up and drool.
Who do you think you are . . .
a human being?

Reeking, rotten, filthy punk,
street mouth spewing slime,
stand up and fight!
I ought to shoot
an apple off your head.

Non-compliant creep,
Disobedient dunce,
where's your patriotic fervor?
You better fall in
and get motivated.

    Taunt him, poke him,
    Tell him his mother's a whore and a slob
    Who messes with door-to-door salesmen,
    And is a poisonous cook.
        If he remains recalcitrant,
        Call in the picadors to probe and to pick
        Nick him just enough
        So he sees the light through the red
        And enraged, he sticks you back.
    Trip him, kick him
    Tell him his old man's a gutter wino-o
    A molester of young children, girls and boys,
    And cheats on his income tax.

If he is still unmotivated,
Call in the goon platoon with the
Orange clubs, and pow!
Teach him to dance the Seal Pup Stomp
And the good old fashioned Bunny Bop.

Oh, First you grab your partner, Start a fight,
Slam him to the left, Bash him to the right
Step upon his body till he sees the light
Then you club again, and smash again with all your might
Make a man of him by spitting in his face
Then you do the Pugil Rock for the human race
Swing your boot 'way 'round, plant it in his back
That's what we call, Training him, Jack.

In an Attic Filled With Someone Else's Childhood

Like unsocketed, sightless eyes,
marbles once spilled here blister the floor
of this haunted chamber.
Two of them—an unmatched glassy pair—stare, then glare
through me, at me.
I am not wanted here, yet am pulled, drawn, suctioned in,
as an old, cold wind whispers behind my back.
I am an unwelcomed, unwarranted presence here,

       an intruder in this other child's space

       and I long for the uneasy comfort of

       my own time, my own place.
In a dusty portrait there's a small dog looking hugged and happy
while the little boy who holds it is stiff, ready to snap.
And way over there, in the darkest corner of this cheerless room
a copper weather vane horse labeled "Temperance"
gallops the gloom.

The Almost One

Choosing the full experience,
I wanted to welcome him with warmth and soft sweet sounds
—not in bleary stupored
dullness while cool impersonal hands handled him—
but whispering "happy birthday" into the tiniest ear,
making our very, very first moment link.

Days of boundless energy, mixed with deepest fatigue;
Darkness a thousand nights long, Sleep fitful, fleeting, light.
Watching over the quickly, slowly growing presence
Feeling tides turn and my small ocean's roll
I squirmed with pleasure-pain when it churned,
And waited with less and more patience for the time to arrive.

Splintering the pre-dawn, the surprising deluge
    (really only a trickle) announced
It's time: Wake up, sweetheart, wake up.
Here we go!

Breathing consciously counting
relaxing between,
Breathing slowly, shallowly
deeply, panting.
It's all right, baby, all right
Only hard work
for both of us
The hardest we'll ever do.

Altered faces hover in the pristine room
Quieted mouths turn quivery sad.
Cool sheathed hands flutter,
wringing themselves helplessly.
"God dammit!" cries someone through a mask
and punches the wall.

Do you want to see him, they ask gently.
No. I might never try again if I were to see
that cord around and around and around,
drawn tighter and tighter as he battled to be born,
strangling him as he reached his moment.

How much more precious are those to come because of you,
My dearest, poorest, almost one?

The Omega Point

Disenfranchised,

his brain a tiny unmade chamber,

his hunger a howling echoing cave,

the Brontosaurus sought sweet succulent dripping greens.

Dimmed dying eyes beseeched the parched depleted landscape.

With small head lowered, with jaw unhinged,

he combed the sand like a primal plow.

He swallowed mouthfuls of acrid dust, bits of wind-honed

gravel raked the serpentine length of his throat.

Disenchanted,

quick-sanded in the substance of his own soul,

the Man hungered still though his belly swelled.

Questioning uneasily the upward outward

thrust from earth to moons to remotest stars,

he somersaulted inward and journeyed to his core.

Finally confronted, Evil writhed in ultimate evolution

imploding in terminal spasm, bursting into reconstituted Good.

Man reached the Omega Point.

California Seascape

The brown seal's body lay there in the morning fog,
quietly bruising the beach
as though a giant shed a muddy teardrop upon the muslin sand.
I stood near the dark stillness and imagined
his baked potato bulkiness lumbering laboriously ashore.

Had an errant, angry wave suddenly scooped up his

life and spat the shell out upon the land?

Was this a suicidal pachyderm, so far out on the

limb of his world that he ended his days

dashed on the outskirts of mine?

Or had he been banished, evicted, or by a rival, ousted

the loser in one of Poseidon's tournaments, out-jousted,

Titan's football punted foully,

finally scrimmaged, kicked out of the game?

But then I saw a small, round hole,
the neat, mean tunnel a bullet had dug
and the seal's stilled presence was clearly explained.
For a stolen fish,
a torn net,
or, worst of all,
maybe just for the hell of it,
one of Neptune's favorite children had been reduced to
an orphaned brown bundle of seaweed and rags.

Colored Lights

Insinuating his body across the boards,

he honky-tonked himself into the spotlight

and my heart,

turning me into a female closet Cyrano,

who'd hide in the folds of the audience's darkness,

trumpeting lust through the nose for that

Rox-Anima-Animus up there on the stage.

And I still journey back in my mind sometimes,

plowing through the gristle and fat,

the girth of the Godfather, the shadowy Kurtz,

burning through that final tango's buttered heat,

reaching at last the pure primal wondrous core

of Stanley Kowalski, Mark Antony, Terry Malloy,

and Bud.

Dolphins: In Embroidery, Symbiosis, Evolution and Show Business

Curved silver needles embroider the sea
Weaving crystal gray threads among the blues and the greens
Satin stitching shafts of moonbeams and sunlight
Into the frothy shimmering tapestry.

The Ethical Pied Pipers with smiling faces
Innocently lead the yellow fin to the cannery,
For the tuna streak toward the gathering nets
Beneath the dolphins' dazzling canopy.
What a tragic symbiotic bargain Neptune struck:
Dolphin pounds of flesh—automatically extracted—
The finders' fee—the price exacted—
Is paid in the fullest by the Shills of the Sea.

Did it all happen in an instant, in one cataclysmic rush?
The seas churned into whirlpools, spewing the others to the dust,
While you milled about the rim of the vortex,
Undulating in fear,
Your warm-blooded heart pounding with intelligent dread?
Did you consider following the others
As they slithered laboriously ashore?
Did you call out to them? Beg them to stay?
Was it inertia? Or simply your own choice?
A loathing of challenge? Or were you opting for life?
Is there—in that large brain of yours—
A secret compartment holding the answers?

Imprisoned behind panes of thick glass
In giant bathtubs, I see you dancing on your tail,
Flying through hoops.
Up close, I must smile at you—and you smile back.
Your precocious babyface could be bonneted,

Your bottlenose beak sucking a soft, pudgy thumb
And I think of dumb, stupid things to say like:
"What's a sweet kid like you
doing in a joint like this?"
Then our eyes meet.
And they lock.
And I am first to look away
Because you have stopped me cold and I feel embarrassed.
For your warm eyes are those of a melancholy clown
With a great crystal tear glued to his chalky cheek.
Suddenly my heart is so deeply touched,
I sink into a small ocean of salty tears.

Dona Quixote

Now bulges and swells

With poltergeist surprises,

With wised up children

And tangled trees.

It's hard to believe in spontaneous events

Now that the inexplicable mysteries

No longer seem so mysterious,

And when endless explanations are provided

For questions one hasn't wanted to ask.

So are windmills really only windmills,

Or has some knave tied a knot in my lance?

Be that as it may, I must venture forth

To plunge deep into an angry sea

Seething with spear carriers,

Armed with my trustiest smile,

Wildly brandishing my butterknife.

The Last Resort
(Hotel del Coronado, San Diego, Ca.)

Unbleached muslin beach
trimmed with dappled blues and greens
stretches taut and wide.
Sailing masts make their point,
exclaiming into a jet-trailed sky.
Palm trees—like the tails of lions—stiff as boards
thrust upward through the sand,
punctuating the same sky.
It is as if colossal lions buried there guard an ancient tomb,
a treasure trove of doubloons and doilies,
uncomic valentines and tea roses,
carefully pressed, dried and mauve.
In altered, swirling, crackling air,
there are wisps and whispers everywhere.
Hand-clasped couples milling, strolling,
white flannel, fringed parasols,
pale chiffon flowing.
Strains of What'll I do? moaned by saxophones
haunt the wind.
Crimson cupolated castles clustered there
doze in deep duned reverie,
dreaming Mohican, Gatsbian dreams,
Leaning genteelly toward the approaching sea.

Chatelaine

Her life,

neither illumined hallway

nor darkened tunnel

with blazing light at the end,

but an intricate, winding passage

lined with doors

    some ajar

    some open

    some locked.

To be tried,

to be opened,

to be entered

or not.

The chatelaine explores the corridors,

Keys to the castle hang at her side.

87 Saviors 87

His birth is foretold
Awaited by a chaotic, troubled world.
He comes gently born
Through a mother who's human,
A father divine.
On a bed of straw, of stone, of moss, of leaves
A tiny benign presence, glowing,
Whose arrival is heralded by a spectacular light in the sky
That leads wise
and worldly men to His side
To observe Him
So they can go to the powers that be
To inform them of His coming.

    He remains to live half a lifetime,

    Speaking, touching, disappearing,

    Into deserts, mountains, vineyards and mist

    Re-emerging to palpitate the senses with messages

    of courage and tenderness,

    Lifting hearts, directing eyes upward,

    Healing, comforting the down-trodden,

    Feeding the ravenous hunger,

    Quenching the desperate thirst.

        And the entrenched are outraged
        And know that they are threatened
        So He is reviled, humiliated,
        Degraded, spat upon
        And put to death most cruelly.

            But He rises,

            For He is Mithra,

            Osiris,

            Adonis,

            Tammuz,

            Jesus,

            And eighty two more.

He's Too Heavy (So He Ain't My Brother)

The Maharishi's paths were strewn with roses
Masking odious odors from desensitized noses.
Nourished limbs assuming the lotus position
Assumed no responsibility for the human condition.
Shriveled arms ending in wooden beggars' bowls
Left no imprint on those injourneying souls.
Disconnectedly standing upon their heads,
Intoning mantra refrains,
They collectively died of hardness of hearts
And terminal, varicose brains.

The Fast Exit

In the event of my untimely death,
should I be yanked out of my life by
runaway horse, lightning bolt,
untended, unbraked truck, or
any other lethal means with right of way;
If you mourn me,
and I hope that you would care terribly
for a while, that I'm gone,
think of this through your tears:

    I shall have had the last breath whacked out of me
    as was the first, whacked in, upon my delivery, brand new.

    I shall have been spared vacant hours, staring at pale
    unmuraled walls, and the jolt of fingers turned to claws,
    no longer capable of flight across the keys.

    I shall have been denied the surprise of invitations
    unextended and grown-up children who seldom appear.

    I shall have been saved the disinheritance of my own
    containment, teeth that remain only to loosen, lean and
    crumble, feet that bunion bony and shuffle along,
    meek murmuring heart whispering complaint within its
    crackable shell, its faint sound roaring in inner ear,
    my voice raised in righteous demand and indignation,
    an echo, a small, raspy, ineffectual croak.

So, you whom I dearly love,
and those of you who may cherish me,
In the event of a most sudden departure,
feel free to gather on the platform to
weep and wave as my train clatters by.
If there's a choice in the matter,
I vow to fight like a Tasmanian devil for possession of my life.
But if I lose the struggle,
the tug o' war,
if the moment slips away from me,
out of my grasp,
It will be the time for remembering what I have told you,
that it could have been much, much worse.

Billy Graham

Billy Graham

billy graham

Trussed up sugared

half-baked ham.

Gucci shod

Honey tressed

Roman threads

Finely pressed.

If God changes his mind

and decides to come back

Billy'll pick him up at the airport

in his Cadillac.

I Liked Louis

At 26, Queen Christina of Sweden abdicated her throne (either to embrace Catholicism or to avoid prosecution for dipping too deeply into the royal till). Mostly on horseback, she traveled to France where she met Louis XIV, then a boy of 16, and his mother. Dusty and dishevelled, Christina strode into the palace hall where she was presented to the Queen Mother of France. Although there's no historical account of this moment as far as I know, from Christina's point of view, perhaps that royal encounter went something like this.

Thick layers of lavendered powder and glistening paint could not
disguise the Queen Mother's instant appraisal of me:

Deformed Spartan, her haughty, baggy eyes seemed to scream,
bass-voiced, flat-heeled, soiled, unpressed, uncombed . . .

But aloud:

"Welcome to France," her unctuous-ness purred, her
bejewelled dragon's paw extended, "Sweden is now bleak
indeed sans your glowing presence, Christina."

Ignoring her dried, amethyst, veiny claw, I sought her
gimlet eyes instead:

"The warmth of your gracious salutation melts this Ice
Queen's heart," I hissed, "and the exquisite beauty of La
Belle France uplifts my soul."

And then, I gave my flannel riding skirts a great thumping
whack with my crop,
freeing an enormous cloud of French dirt and dust
which enveloped the Queen Mother completely,
making the nasty old dragon cough and sneeze.

But oh, I so liked Louis,
that young and handsome sunny King,
and on sight, I could tell he liked me as well.
Such a spirited, willowy, loving boy,
filled with elegance, brimming with grace.

That evening, entranced, I watched Louis dance
with his beloved cousin.
As one, they were, a beautiful blur of satin brocade,
openly adoring each other as they whirled 'round and
'round the marble floor.
Observing the hooded eye of the Queen Mother slithering
after them,
once again, I read her thoughts and knew
that the inability to love brings forth cold, cold
hatred for those who do.

Jean-Jacques Rousseau

Wildly flapping windmill mind

flailing,

impaling himself

upon his own words, his own deeds.

He bleeds.

Mon Dieu, how he bleeds!

Inside the Cat

My humans watch comic images on a television screen
While I sit on the mantle watching the real thing:

    The family sheepdogs
    Laurel & Hardy in dog suits
    Two gentle bumpkins
    Roughnecking each other in prime time.

The porcelain clock tick ticks beside me
As I gaze upon two furry peasants frolicking below.
Oh see the village idiots jousting on the carpet,
Behold the trolls rolling on my palace green.
I do smile upon such jolly jesters
for they do so tickle the crown.
Six year old canines—that's forty two—
Persisting in perpetual puppyhood
Grandmas in hot pants
Codgers in swaddling,
Big Bird and Cookie Monster
in shaggy drag.
They're a sweet pair of scruffy clowns,
tripping over their own bagginess
and their long, pink tongues.
Tails like baseball bats, breakers of ashtrays,
collectors of dust
While mine a scepter, a plume, conductor of symphonies.

    For they are beer, I am Beaujolais
    They are Channel 13, I am PBS
    Tap Dancers, Ballet.
    They bounce, I glide
    They are one plus one, I am infinity.
    They grovel, I stare,
    They beg, I ask.
    They slobber,
    I never.

Portrait of a Butterfly

If you need an analyst,
steer clear of butterflies
for analysis is the task of taking things apart,
of meticulously cataloging each minute complexity in sequence,
thus enabling a sure and safe return.

So, asking a butterfly to be analytical
is like engaging an infant to overhaul your transmission,
or a webfooted gargoyle to plead your case.
It's like hiring a puppy to guard the palace,
which is unheard of,
like a gourmet chef overcooking an egg,
or requiring a performing seal to lay one.

Any lepidopterist worth his salt knows full well
butterflies are not particularly intense.
But they are terrific flitterers and flutterers
and they know all the current songs and dances.
They shop around a lot but purchase little.
If you're awaiting a bus and it's driven by a butterfly,
better call a taxi because that bus may not stop.
Butterflies do not come equipped with heavy machinery.
They light on things
Effortlessly,
which makes their departure, therefore,
Effortless, too.

Now, ants are well known to be industrious
and may quite possibly be analytical.
With the exception of drones and queens,
all bees are activists.

In an analytical world of insects,
there was once a praying mantis named Freud
who was often extremely destructive to his clientele.
He had a waiting room full of beetles and lady bugs
but never, ever a butterfly.

The Last Rite

There was an odd questioning expression in his half-masted
agnostic eyes.
Was my reading right—that he sought the final sacrament—
or was the feeling I had something welling up from a deep
place in me,
and not from his dying eyes at all?
Was he preparing ultimate confrontation with possible God,
or was the bombardment of approaching death so swift, so intense
that all thought vibrated, loosened, blurred,
short circuiting his enlightened philosophical mind?
Was there one slender thread of quiet, slippery peace,
or must the death of a giant be a fluorescent pinwheel,
whirring hypnotically,
spraying sparks,
all known colors,
spinning, spinning,
wresting breath away,
all light in disordered universe
shrinking steadily,
reducing to a single, unverified star,
to a pinhole,
to a quasar,
to an essence
in me.

Poems by

William Wallis

Before Sunrise

The earth whirls about the sun,
The night's run shifts toward light;
I drift suspended in the swing
Below my son's bedroom window.
I hear him toss in sleep, moan,
And begin the long wrestle
In his filmic depth with some scaled shadow.
I know the old forms turning in him.
My motion is comic, calm,
My dreams hang heavy
In my own vast museum.
I would like to fall to the earth's center
And study all this in stillness,
But it is not still there, either.

Trees arch above
And above that arcing,
Star sheets wrap.
Enclosed by a sliding geometry of force,
I could slip inward where
Dark winds would bind me to a shifting surface
And hidden lines burrow under me.
Time might crush me but for
The slow pendulum of his dreaming breath—
My little god of leaves and calculus.
Hard curving, he moans,
Haunted by dark seeds
Stirring deep in his garden.
Let the morning come.
We'll be here, suspended
In swing and sleep,
Caught in the greater dance.

St. Stephen's Square, Vienna

Asher at four months stands steady on my reclining torso,
Watches the autumn crowd blur by. I see only him.
Gradually he tires, aims his layered bulk
To fall heavy on my chest, then clamors up
Toward the silver coins of my spectacles.
We come face to face, the crowd distant.
Then tiny fingers clasp at my face,
Rough temples, plop fingertips
On slit lids, tweak jug handle ears,
Honk my nose—then he leans
Casually into my mouth.
Cheek to cheek, we lovers stay a while
Drifting alone, until his arms slip
And he falls deeper yet, into sleep.
I consider the color washed sky
While above us rise the graceful dimensions of St. Stephen's,
Line upon line interweaving in ascension,
Matrimonie of form and purpose
Signifying harmony.
A need beyond understanding
Has settled here in waking stone.
Here, where my son's sweet pulse is my own.
Let me know your face,
Let me know your eyes.
Come, Asher, look up now from dream
As longing rises in stone,
And silent forms stream by us below.
Whisper to me from sleep, dear son,
Here in the spires' shadow,
Tell us how we may all touch each other
Deeper than this stoney flesh allows.

All Sons

It is near noon; all morning I've fought
To retain a map, even a sketch
Of last night's surging dream.
In a daylight urge that unwraps
The folds of my day's work,
I relive the faded roots of that vision.
You and Dad are with me, Asher;
You raise a horizon hand, sign expansion
Of color, and sea-like movement of form.
Our arms joined, we rise
From shore into sea air,
Toward a bright flux.

Then there are two fragments, Asher:
Your excited laughter (as when we create,
Then name animals with sound and gesture),
And your tiny hand buried in my father's fist
Before my encompassing arms.
I believe
The cause of ascent
Was our interlocked arms,
From which came a lifting,
The upward curving motion
Of endless lines containing
All sons.

Dream Son

The shadow of your absence cools my chest.
Far from you, I fall back. My arms trace your form,
My thoughts slacken, cling to a jagged pulse.
I align our drifting beds in separate places.
You came from broken sighs and limb's moan.
We wrestled you new from old races, our forms
Yours when restless we danced you from a dream.
We woke, and knew we were no longer alone.
Buried then, now filling sunlit rooms, your
Eggshell head hovers between the dream expanse
Of earth and light-rich sky. And now your dancing
Flight to me shatters barriers unlearned.
    In this endless moment's tumble to white sleep
    I promise to keep this fragile rite of the lonely.

Son and Father

Asher at four
winds in furious motion
string about his bike, pausing
now and again to study the web
dense at the center frame
sprocketting out to wheel and projecting bars.
I'm giving it a motor, he says.
(See? his over-the-shoulder
glance echoes.)
I sit nearby spinning my own cycles
as my angel creates his world
from string and steel
and fire of heaven.

Hummingbird

After so long, there you quickly are!
Vibrant hummer! My blind gaze had
Forgotten your possibility,
Had settled on every solid appearance but you.
Now you hover, curling
The only dimension left me, your cool pulse
Melts the leaves and lawn into a restless surface.
Pure geometry of the air,
Pinprick dream, flyfall of ecstasy—
Naming will not make you more real.
Stay—I feel your impossible quickness on my face.
Part of me will go with you—
Your wings are pure.
Is all this bent matter
A shadow of your home?
As you shape this yard with infinite beats
Above my spectacles of space and time,
Transmit to me your succinct truth.
Here, in this deep fold of reality,
Leave the dark indenture of your form
To hover in me. Then disappear,
Awful beauty.

Five Haiku

Rich falling sky,
the moon fades in—
poor poet torn from earth.

Pale moon
over ruddy earth—
poet presses hands together.

Moon shudders, slips
from cloud casing—
aching, the poet turns.

Pale morning sky,
oval moon—
poet mourns the light.

Pale sky, pale moon—
invisible tides
wash the earthbound poet.

Allerseelen

Your eyes were beetles, ebony brilliant,
Your strong jaw narrowed by rage within,
Your hair thick as in that last year you
Returned from there to a scattered family.
When you came to me last night, truepenny—
Gentle, grasping as I never knew you
Capable—we could only gesture through
Dense smoke, *What, are you here?* Then I began
To speak incessantly, told you all I am
And am not, the hate and fear you taught me,
The pain of forced freedom, how alike yes
We are in bone and thought—but you cried out
   An unending word that broke my voice
   With darkness, pain, and lack of choice.

Clearing

Enclosed in woods, we worked close, alone.
The pond was at our back; a mist hid our faces.
Your ax hewed the air near my head—then again!
I fell down from you, stunned empty by fear.
Our eyes did not meet. An empty fury
Circled above us, backed me out of the space
Bared by our work. My eyes pierced your back.
You attacked the woods again, betrayed.
Had you glimpsed the distance between our souls
And released an ancient gesture of rage
And fear in your late labor's dark dance?
Should I have stilled my fear, Dad, bowed my head
To your wild will, and waited for the flame
In that clearing overgrown with failed love?

On the Death of a Colleague

Yes, he is dead and soon enough his
Image will withdraw from our repertoire;
A few gestures (or a pose) will remain laser-clear,
Pulsing in a vague arena within us,
    but beyond our near chronology.

But no matter how we tinker or bend our art,
He has gone—changed scenes, careening—
Exited breathless where we will not
Freely go. Nor motion to him from the stage,
    signing embarrassed, "I was sorry to see you . . ."

Still, we remain and nights when we lie in sleep
Above him, our bones shift to align with his;
And in the earth's turn and wheel's spin,
Who knows what force may bring me
    over the arch and closer to him.

Had I loved him as I do you, dear friend,
I would wish him flight, as the hawk dreams
Wingless its path; I had dreamed him
A needle-nosed jet's ascent
    into the sky's cool wash.

I wish him the stillness words never left him
While he stalked among us. Now he is free from
His flesh's angular drive, the fear of a fine mind's fall.
What can we know of him now, caught as we are
    in continual motion?

I can say that, driven, he wrote a young man's prose,
That his words will live longer than most of us;
That he was infrequently cruel. Peak through the curtain,
See his final acts: like my father's, in service
    to a dark theater only he knew.

Father's Day

Early summer light gathers up the yard's diverse elements.
Unites the myriad moving entities in a vibrating blanket of color.
In the vine and grass tapestry my son reels in golden joy,
Romps about the lawn while I tend roses before the house.
Enclosed in this lattice of light and time
We write in action: Asher's furious dance is pure energy;
My old husbandric ideas are of my young dad,
Arms great and voice echoing in these kneeling hours.
Thorned vines clutch at my wrist, drawing blood
And chilling like the cold roots that writhe
Beneath near green memory.
Buzzing deep beneath this dank screen of the constructed past,
The mind digs alone toward chaos
With its pattens of current and flame.
Certain pictures are the beginning of order,
And knowledge of them the root of calm.
In my self are the surest roots
Because they rest in my father's heart,
And bear the flower circling this yard.
These roots are calm, hardly stirring,
And deep and calm as this bud resting
Between my rough fingers. I know this bud
By my immediate perception of its living parts,
The sensual oneness of its folded essence,
And the impression of its wholeness on me—
Yet you are no less real to me than it, father.

There, I place it in me on the same sturdy shelf.
I feel its resilience and know its image as I know
The curve of my son's sweet head.
There, now the shelf is filled with you three.
Here in this yard, bright signature of my inner world—
While my boy spins, crying out joyful—
I voyage restless through the roses
Where happiness stalks with
The renowned opportunism of the cat.
Then I am left breathless
By a sudden great rose
Suspended before the stucco wall
Green laced yet burning free
Strong as Dad's hand
Broad as my son's face
Floating in the even light,
And my heart strikes bright in untamed bond
With nature, linked with father's love,
While all around me living and dead forms whirl.
I stand rooted in the sun carpet, taunting
The envelope of darkness below
Summer's early song of light and memory.

Nebraska

Those years mowing dry yards in west Lincoln
Left crabgrass memories, a clutching hatred
Of sharp white fences and shrill narrow gates,
Of thrifty chats hinting at sandy mouths.
Flat land spreads guilt thin, as summer's sluggish
Thigh drifts listless on the soil's loose sheets.
Intensity and glow fade from the pale child's
Dusty piping for a sense of place.
Nebraskaland is bruised with fields of sand,
Its culture worn cropless by dull lust.
A nation's oldest dream fades in the hands of
Fourth generation mechanics of the earth's crust.
    Still, the child can see the horizon rear,
    Crust with cloud jewels, rain blood and fear.

Caliban

Bound, I scream soundless in fury, my enclosure
crushing me as I sense rapid movement above.
Writhing still in frozen layers, claws and fins
poised sharp I sense a slight give upward.
Ready, my sinew howls out for freedom
From the icy clay enclosing me.
I smell the foul damp of the riverbottom—
my hearts are calmed by thoughts of its moisture,
my numberless tiny teeth stir.
Dreaming, I drive a great limb into warm water
and scream into weakened earth.
My glacier tongue writhes in stone and coal,
as my arm pulls my shoulder and head from iron mud.
Emerged slimy from the earth bottom
I am washed and pry with my claws
the itching bulbs open to pain.
Ah, cold light!
Molish, I study through slits
grey green shadows running away.
Movement and dance!
Free elements, blue and light.
I pull up my hinderparts, stretch,
crouch stone-heavy in the current.
Fish dart from me like mad particles.
Then on the floor before me—
What? A form of grey light shimmers.
It must come from—Ah
light above! Gathering, searing down!
With winged movement she flicks across the surface,
embraces the liquid plane, quick
her wonderful form dances in rhythmic
patterns. The elements gather
about her, signs of the air in their wake.
Fluid pulses in my trembling lungs.
I am born.

Landscape with Clouds

The long cold front
lingers on mountained horizons
boiling with incomplete forms struggling
out of formlessness tossed headlets swell up
grey from earth in fetal glory up out of the sea
greatbacked beasts monstrous felines weasels
struggling arching nameless indescribable
crawling about writhing plateaus
below then from the complex
generation the head widens
expands earward bottom
falls inward the clean
neck narrows
atmosphere
violates form
complete in that
instant the agony of failed
birth finally clear the sweet expansion
and contraction of sure science, prayer now
violated the lifting of cold fronts from us empty meta-
morphosis of earth from Eden to cloud chamber
with neverending loss of vision

and ah below the falling

Pacific Coast Fragments
July 1989

Crushed against
the wild freedom of the coast, I know
far out from these shores my lover settles deeper
in her cool bed, shifting, spreading,
as my children slip toward consciousness.
The sea ripples cold,
splits to waves
as pearly light
strikes the ebbing surface of things.

White noise outside the car's steel bubble
sifts in as something elderly
cracks, shifts its hidden features,
surrenders to a fitful mirror.
Last night's whispers replace
the seashell's ancient moan.

The '52 dumpster's squat power
fills the road, grim, sudden.
The wheeling slug sighs,
shrugs knowingly as I pass.
Unblinking it
puffs rancid, cabbagelike
in rear view. Its ancient gears
scream ruin on the early California coast.

It coughs, falls back,
exhausted, exploding—
ancient victim of the roads.
Slick, young, I sweep on
secure in power and intuition,
but the stench begins to penetrate
metal, glass, plastic—
piercing all secure things.

Tears unannounced.
This cold lava
was once moth wings.

Finally,
you accept the impulse to
cut your hair short.
You draw me deep
in your liquid mouth,
I thrust my lips to yours,
our spines reversed we
converse in lost tongues.
Two electric strands writhe slow,
new silence is born.

The long miles pass calmly by.
I scream alone in my car.
Singer, there is no place for your song.
Sing for these cliffs
like Art to the East River,
like Bird in Camarillo.
Hey, it's okay.

I miss you.
        You are now
the pale form
at the last dark turn.
All we never said
        I must invent,
half in love, half insanity.
        Mother,
your quick, true son sees
the cloud wisps of your gown
as they are pulled into
the coast's dark cliffs.

Yet it was simply
meant to be.
All this and more.

Youth burns by
a motorcycle flings itself past,
wasplike, stinging the dense salt air.

The biker's death drifts,
comes quick—
ah slick dark curve unwinding.

Pop music: the dream
and virus of travelers.

Returning,
the coast foggy and cold.
Remember you have lost friends
on this road.
Turn inland where
the road is straight, predictable,
where it doesn't matter that
there is too much of everything.

The unsubtle rub
of fighting this road
with its dry roar
of endlessly passing things
deadens if you don't fight,
if you accept its perpetual motion.
No, not this way
of white noise, eyes
numb points fixed dead on an electric grid,
where lines and dots mean only numbers
and the shapes of numbers.
Better roar into emptiness
and scream silent into
this endless map of the real.

Begin now—
senses distended,
soul numb, face down,
but straining up,
moaning truth
into the fitful roadbed.

Shells Seabound

No beauty laces their serrated edge.
Scuffed and rust stained in spreading lines,
Grey ledges widen out to echo earth motion.
These two shapes, more stone than sand,
More collapsing earth than prying ocean lip,
Fell once in sudden violence into each other,
Were welded with heat enough to warp nature's curve.

Beyond original intent or function,
In rough fusion of unlikely partners,
These cracked, drying veins lapped and spread
On this surface, an asymmetrical accident—
A minor mote, listless as algae's song—
As your eye chanced to find their union,
Laced it with remembrance of passion,
And took it from the sandscape,
As we take each other from the world
In rocking motions of the sea.

And if on some future shore our forms should be found
Crushed inseparate as these, and wound in patterns
Of wind and wave, what power could divine
Our love, our sea birth beyond drowning?

Song

All forms settle into yours,
fragrant hair softly restive,
cloudlike in the even dark breeze;
luxurious eyes under cool brow—
lakelight plays there in silky depth;
sweet, exquisite lips purse,
shape soundless motion; a glow
floods over evening's broad back.

I draw the pliant body, perfect
pear breasts ivory and gold,
stems coral tipped,
belly swelling velvet ripe.
Languorous back falls to full
lush smoothness of limb.
Your body,
juncture of motion and stillness,
pulsing and still,
inclines to mine
to know the chosen chaos
of waking desires,

sleeping desires,
the formless longing
after all forms.

Dream

Hung in a noose of light descending
in soft weight clinging limbs wound
fast we hover in space between
birth and that which follows.

Hair interwound,
eyes ebony deep clasp the motion
silken thighs insistent, we fall
complete lips bellies locked

There can be no end; we tumble
past hands fingers nails cells
bare particulars, motivations, atoms
lost movement, the illusion of motion

Then there is
disintegration into palatial
nothingness, crushing silence
that will draw endless

lines free of gravity.
Laughter the only wound,
I awaken cool erect,
hands hungry, soul distended.

In the Theater

you stir, profile of light
inclined as lights fade

music breathes from you cloudlike
while from the deep garden of instruments

sounds arise, turn away mysterious,
your scent, dress, glance arranges

the turgid air in patterns of ecstasy
your hand stirs, veined ivory

brushes shoulder, your form
shudders, caught in sound's web

the past rises into future
I wake as the stage lights stir

from the dream of waking
the music of your morning arms.

Landscape

Let the past be and fall away, and after
clothes settle in clouded fields below you,
fall back slow into the eternal forms
we become here where lovers are.
Shadows cling to curves dovetailing,
melodies of flesh circle out
from an opening sigh. I kneel
before breasts weighty, veined
splendor to gather and cry out for,
infant lover drawing up darkened flesh.
You fall spread, your lower lips the only
worthy idea left in this little universe.
Spinegathering, the folds part
pearling as you drift clouded back
into another country, your journey signaled
by a faint smile of fading consciousness. Your
arms settle, rise, shape a shield of freedom.
And the map of our garden pleasure
with rich sweet hedges and fragrant plants
blossoming leafy, hillocks rippling,
this ivory landscape pulses, shifting splendor
centers my vision in the ripe nexus
opening beneath your crimson pulse.

Sweet friend mounted, deep reed in wind,
all my strength yours,
all my time lost in our joining, all
my swollen need caught, grasped
in your ecstatic moment.
In this bent circle we
share cloud with earth.
Airy map of heaven stretched
beneath me, sigh out dark stars
as I fly—breath torn,
wings steady—through a vision
never seen before yet always there—
pliant strength bent wavelike
under rough weight, receiving what
earth offers sea and mist at dawn,
the landed thrust of love in arms.
Now fall back deeper in sleep and see
the rub of velvet sand on wave
will not cease in dream.

Cadillac

Our night boat rocks
        calm, insistent
on a hidden street
        sidling
your soft
        laughter free
mantic with sighs
        hisses
build
        dark waves
crashing soft against
        our origin
in dream
        The city
folds away
        as you slip
back, falling spread
        legs lips
velvet fragrance surges
        in side
street ecstasy
Fretful tugs, jagged
        lip lock
beneath fogged windows
        in the first
wave of rhythmic
        expansion

Blind eyes focus
        lost memories
melodies far away
        begin
somewhere beyond the visible
        humming beasts
in slow procession
        toward us

swimming up
        the earth
gather now about the car
        within it swans
and darting fishes
        circle golden
about you gasping
        while my
hungry mouth circles
        among folds
pulsing furrows, flesh
        yields, expands
hisses its sweet air
        from arguing
the taut stretching
        of joy in
flesh subsiding
        in joy
We pause kissing
        proper lips
Your eyes silken
        in passing headlights
shine deep into
        my dark
You slip down, swan
        drawn, then the
licking, kissing suck
        grip of lips
about my head
        lip shiver
of body swallowed
        down
the black
        swan draws
you swirling
        hair into
pools of mutual
        ecstasy

speaking in tongues
         deep babble
we thrash in the sea
         stretching from us
to out there where ships
         sail lost
and back
         Ah the swift current
the ocean bed
         dark shock cool
from far beneath
         the explosive
yes

Then slow siren drag
         of buried
flood invisible
         brief as
the perfect white
         of your eye
fluttering in the current
         of restive sea
settling back in
         ocean drift

The painfully beautiful woman
         bows to the worshipful man.
In the last ceremony of darkness
         cadillac thrusts into the night.

This is how death, the air, works

Come, little bird, stop circling a moment and settle
here in my arms, and listen to your father who loves you.
These two roses in the early light—yes, you
hold this fresh blossom, and I'll hold the other.
Grasp gently or they'll draw their color from you.
You see, smell, feel these sweet machines.
We know this garden in spring, know
how this stem was drawn up out of the earth,
silently pushed from the dark motion below the grass.
(This is the same dark force
that drives dream through us
as we lie buried in our sandy beds.)
In night the rose rises up to bud,
the night's secrets folded within it.
It rises above the grasping foliage,
and opens to the sun
as the inky sheets of night
purple, then pull themselves west.
In the first light the bud stirs,
then springs slowly open, just as your
green eyes dance beneath their lids
to signal inner light before you
are lifted from the sleeproad
to blossom in the air, brighteyed,
petalcheeked, bursting with life.
    No, stay with me, and listen a moment.
Soon I'll be silent and you can run and play.
Touch this smoothness,
these flames of earth ecstasy.
See how petals explode from the tiny bulb
in radiant fragrance, to breathe the light.
This is a mask of God, Asher,
smiling at us in symmetry.

And this second rose,
You see how these petals wilt and drift,
turning to earth in the early breeze
to mix with grass and dust
to sink in growing stillness
to become free in the dark currents of earth—
where new petals will begin their rise.
This is the mystery: how beauty grows
from dark, reveals itself a moment,
then returns through air to earth.
It is the language of earth and air,
and old sunlight.
    Now, listen, little angel. My mother is sick.
Soon we'll fly together to see her.
She is like this second rose, thin,
her skin as dry as these faded petals,
and she is pale.
Soon, she too will fall and go down to earth
like this pallid fragrance.
And then she will linger in the memory
of those who loved her
and whom she loved:
we who can read her life's symmetry,
as we study roses on mornings like these.
This is the lesson the garden teaches.
This is how death, the air, works.
From this sweet fullness to this wilted frame
is the way of all things.
Yet it goes slowly and we trace
the color and original motion
of each part of the thrusting up and fall.

So, little one, these father bones
will encircle you in this garden,
and protect you for a time from certain dangers.
Still, the air's old burning
will pull us from the dark and spin us down again.
In this bright flame, I will also wither,
these strong hands fail,
but not until yours are strong
and encircle a child to take my place.
Here, now, take the first rose,
my mother's youthful cheek,
my own youth, now your own.
You, the blossom of your mother's flesh,
Go, fly up now, and circle high!
I release your springing quickness.
I will live now in the bouquet of your breath
which has, in these few glancing years,
caught me deep within my own circling.

First Form

```
            sunSpun
           eyes spark
           honey lips
              neck
             angelic
noble           shoulders
up    full breasts  up
p   Jut Vibrant    er
ar      waist      m
low  spinal grace  er
a  cherubic hips  rm
   full  fra  grant
   ah   secret   ah
   velvet     thighs
   full &    & fine
    long      legs
   sweet     knees
   firmc     alves
    ank      les
   fawn      feet
   10tin    ytoes
```

Of the Few Things I Do Know

I know how the Devil will appear.
He will sit prim and quiet in the class rear.
For him there will be no answers; his objections
Will be unspoken, echoed by a quick glance out the window,
Yet crystal clear. The class will be confused
By his pointed silence. In the computer room
He will somehow ruin each naive printout, but
Subtly—with the mere press of a single digit,
Of dry substance on plastic.
Then glitches will worm their way
Through the grids of expensive programs. Confessional
Writing will vanish in a flick. The mind will
Be desecrated as he strokes his thin blond beard,
Seemingly puzzled at tears, head atilt in sympathy,
Eyes averted in the knowledge of toadstools
And machine-like creatures running backward,
Pausing only to regain their balance,
In slippery fields outside the window
His glance has inured with chaos.

Transfiguration

Did you see yourself
through a dark mirror
those last days?
Did a new
spirit infect you,
inconsolable mother?

Emaciated, you surged frail
about the barred bed,
to and from me, a
restless sail of skin and bones.
What fear, what quiet
was in those gaunt eyes
focused on distant things—
vague realities of Chance
(the goddess of the unspoken
awful indifferences),
or a late reaction to
possible emptiness
behind the shifting light.

Sweet Mom.
         Then you
surged outward in sleep,
to drift peacefully.

You are free,
and in the bright dream is
no more fight for breath,
no more seizure and shame,
no more half life,

but wing on wing
undespairing
into eternity,
gentle sailor,

the only thought
the fullness beyond.

The Poets

Born 53 years ago in the midwest but "raised" in Los Angeles on 15 years of newspaper editing, **Michael Marth** calls himself enculturated, illiterate, revolutionary, mad, and raw. He is Dad, ninth man of nine on a running young Monday night basketball team and co-founder laureate of the Eternally Poets' Society, an ongoing workshop. He has produced a chapbook and three volumes of poetry: *Hanging On By My Tongue*, *Fiendish*, and the latest still in longhand tentatively titled *Sketches of the Fool on the Hill*.

Terence Martin was born in England and raised in Los Angeles. He is a musician and an English teacher, currently playing in clubs in the Los Angeles area and teaching at Valley College. His poetry has appeared in such magazines as *Maelstrom Review* and *Angel's Flight*, and he has read his poems on cable television. He lives in Van Nuys, California.

A.C.L. Stanton is Ann Stanton, wife and mother, writer of poetry and prose. After a career in television production, she and her husband, Allen, transplanted themselves and their two children from New York to California. In spite of smog, gridlock, and runaway development, to Ann, this part of the country still represents those wider open spaces in which her interests and imagination feel freer to roam. The poems in this collection appeared in *Manuscript*.

William Wallis teaches English and Humanities at Valley College and lives in Los Angeles with his wife Leslie and sons Asher and Joshua. He has two previous volumes of poetry: *Poems* (Blue Stem Press, 1972) and *Biographer's Notes* (Yellow Barn Press, 1984). His libretto, *Hanblecheya, A Vision*, was set by composer Richard Moore and performed for the U.S. Bicentennial.